Montpellier Travel Guide

Sightseeing, Hotel, Restaurant & Shopping Highlights

Thomas Austin

Copyright © 2014, Astute Press
All Rights Reserved.

No part of this publication may be reproduced, stored in a retrieval system, or transmitted, in any form or by any means without the prior written permission of the publisher, nor be otherwise circulated in any form of binding or cover other than that in which it is published and without similar condition being imposed on the subsequent purchaser.

If there are any errors or omissions in copyright acknowledgements the publisher will be pleased to insert the appropriate acknowledgement in any subsequent printing of this publication.

Although we have taken all reasonable care in researching this book we make no warranty about the accuracy or completeness of its content and disclaim all liability arising from its use

Table of Contents

Montpellier 6
   Culture 8
   Location & Orientation 9
   Climate & When To Visit 10

Sightseeing Highlights 12
   Odysseum District 12
      Planetarium Galilee 13
      Aquarium Mare Nostrum 13
      Karting & Bowling 14
      Ice Skating 14
      Odysseum Activities 15
   Fabre Museum 15
   Montpellier Zoo 16
   Château Flaugergues 17
   Royal Square of Peyrou 18
   St. Peter's Cathedral 19
   Château de La Mosson 20
   Museum of Anatomy & the Faculty of Medicine 21
   Montpellier Historical Centre 22
   Henri Prades Museum 23
   Antigone District 24
   Botanical Gardens 25
   Château de la Mogère 26
   Esplanade Charles de Gaulle 27

Recommendations for the Budget Traveller 28
   Places to Stay 28
      Montpellier Hostel 28
      Les Arbousiers 30
      La Farigoule 31
      La Vagance 32
      Sweet Home 34 32
   Places to Eat & Drink 33
      Playfood 33
      Le P'tit Mas 34
      Le Pescator 34

    Pain et Cie 35
    Times Café 36
Places to Shop **36**
    Les Halles Castellane 36
    Peyrou Plaza 37
    Images du Demain 38
    Le Boutik'R 38
    Etat d'Ame 39

Montpellier

Montpellier is the main city of the Languedoc-Roussillon region in southwestern France and is located only 200 minutes from Paris by high-speed TGV train. It is cosmopolitan city for its size and high-end shoppers love to visit centre-ville.

The city covers 60km^2 and is built on two hills, with the highest point being Place de Peyrou at 57 metres. The two hills, Montpellier and Montpelliéret, and the narrow streets give a cosy feel to this ancient city.

The River Letz winds through the city on its way to the Mediterranean Sea some 16 kilometres distant and the port of Lattes. Montpellier found fortune in the 13th century when Jewish and Arab traders arrived bringing with them silk, spices and sugar. The same trading partners taught the students and merchants of Montpellier a great deal about the world as well as Arabic medicine.

In 1181 Lord Guilhem VIII declared that medicine could be taught by anyone in the city and so the Medical College was born. In the occidental world it is still the oldest operating medical school in the world.

This once sleepy and quiet French city has changed more in the last four decades that it did in the previous three centuries. In the 1960's when 15,000 Algerians fled to France to escape persecution in their own country they descended on Montpellier.

The idyllic existence of the residents was suddenly awakened by the vibrant energy of individuals who were used to the noise and colour of Arab markets. They set about injecting their own lifestyle into the laid-back French way of life and work and helped bring prosperity to the city.

The city is lighthearted and friendly and is fast overtaking Marseille and Nîmes as the best place to live or visit on the coast of southern France. It attracts students in their thousands and it can sometimes be hard to find anyone that was actually born locally. Montpellier has an excellent reputation for being a high-tech town and attracts many computer and technology experts. In the mid 1960's IBM opened their largest European site there.

Culture

The capital of the Languedoc Roussillon area is arguably the most elegant spot on the south coast and certainly pulls in the holidaymakers, nearly 20,000 visitors come to Montpellier every year. This super French city offers more than wonderful architecture, shady traffic-free plazas and boulevards. There is a history and culture with the added bonus of the beach and sparkling Mediterranean Sea only a short drive away.

Modern, chic wine bars, electronic music, designer boutiques and galleries abound to cater for the younger set but there are still more than enough bars, shops and restaurants for the rest of the residents and tourists alike. Take a walk through the city by starting at Place du Comédie then go up rue de la Loge into L'Ecusson where halfway along is the Place Jean-Jaurés. A little further on is Place Marché Aux Fleurs and these are two of the best and busiest places for some people-watching over an aperitif as the sun goes down.

The city is busy and has an energetic feel to it, helped along by the 20% of the population who are students. The academic year is busy but in some ways the best to time to visit as festivals and exhibitions bring colour and excitement to the city.

Mid-June to Mid-July hosts the Le Printemps des Comédiens which is a live entertainment based festival with up to 25 shows of music, culture and circus events. June and July are busy months as the Montpellier Dance festival is in June and the Le Festival de Radio-France et de Montpellier is a music festival in late July. For film buffs the Festival du Cinéma Méditerranéen is in the second half of October and the beginning of November.

Location & Orientation

The city of Montpellier in a few kilometres inland from the Mediterranean Sea on the south coast of France and is halfway between the Spanish and Italian borders, 700 kilometres south east of Paris. There has always been a significant Spanish population and the influence of this can be seen all over the city.

The capital of the Languedoc Roussillon region has seven official districts; divided into sub-districts each with its own council. Ranking 15th in the biggest metropolitan list in France the city population in 2009 was 255,080 with 550,000 in the whole area. It is the fastest growing city in France and the third largest on the Mediterranean coast after Nice and Marseille. In the city itself 43% of the population is under the age of 30.

For getting to Montpellier from other countries there is an airport four kilometres from the city centre. Flights to London are available all year round with seasonal flights from other UK destinations. The Montpellier – Méditerranée Airport offers flights to major airports within Europe as well as to Madeira and North Africa.

The public transport in the city is managed by Transports de l'agglomération de Montpellier (TaM), who look after the parking facilities in the city and the four lines of the tramway. The trams are brightly painted and easy to spot as they glide through the streets. The main railway station is Gare St. Roch which is a stone's throw from the Place Du Comédie and the heart of the city. High-speed TGV trains depart from Montpellier to all of the main stations in France.

The tourist office sells the Montpellier CITY card for €20, this allows free use of public transport and free entry into some of the main attractions.

Getting around Montpellier is easy and if your hotel is close to the station why not take a walk in the sunshine. Alternatively there are buses and taxis or why not hire a bicycle. The Vélomagg bike sharing scheme started in 2007 and there are 50 bike stations and 1200 bicycles.

Climate & When To Visit

Montpellier has a Mediterranean climate that is mild with dry, hot summers and moderate winters but there can be wide seasonal differences.

Spring is lovely and the weather can be pleasant with warm sunny days. This time of year is ideal for sightseeing as it is not too hot and there are fewer crowds. Daytime temperatures reach a high of 21°C with a low of 5°C. In summer the weather can get really hot but the ocean breeze from the Mediterranean Sea helps make the climate more comfortable. For beach lovers a high of 29ªC is great for a lazy day sunbathing. A low of 14° is pleasant for taking a stroll round in the evening and sitting down with a chilled glass of wine, French of course.

Autumn can be great but the temperature drops quickly midway through the season. The high of 15°C at the start of the season very quickly dives down to a low of 5°C as winter approaches. The Christmas season brings with it a high of just 12°C and a chilly low of 1°C. For ski lovers there are many resorts within approximately three hours drive of Montpellier.

MONTPELLIER TRAVEL GUIDE

Sightseeing Highlights

Odysseum District

www.aquariummarenostrum.fr
www.planetarium-galilee.montpellier-agglo.com/
www.centre-commercial-odysseum.com/

There is so much to do at the Odysseum that there might not be time to sit down but if you need to rest you weary feet find the large open arena-style area.

This central point is a good meeting place or you can just sit and relax in the company of statues of historical figures. De Gaulle, Churchill, Mao, Ghandi, Mandela and Golda Meir are just a few of the famous names round the arena. With the brightly painted buildings and palm trees rustling in the breeze the Odysseum has a feeling of Florida, especially when the sky is blue and the sun is shining.

The access is easy straight of the A9 motorway and there are 2050 parking spaces, with the first two hours being free of charge. The tram also runs to Odysseum from the city centre. Tramline 1, the blue tram with white birds, terminates at this fun-filled site, unique in this part of France.

In the commercial centre there are over a hundred shops with all the famous brand names for fashion and home you would expect to find, including Casino Geant, a very large hypermarket. The shops in the commercial centre are open from 10am to 8pm Monday to Saturday and the hypermarket is open slightly longer from 9am to 9pm, again Monday to Saturday.

Planetarium Galilee

The 156 seater theatre with its semi-circular screen allows you to be totally enveloped by the stars and planets that wrap around our Earth. There are different presentations and events including ones especially for children. For anyone keen to learn more about space travel there are reconstructions and documentaries about space travel and astronauts.

There are several exhibitions and a shop for those essential space related souvenirs. The Planetarium opens from 1.30pm onwards and is open every day in the school holidays. Other weeks it is open at weekends and Wednesdays. The admission price is €7 for adults and €6 for children to the Planetarium. There are many special events on and the times and prices do vary.

Aquarium Mare Nostrum

One of the tanks in here measures an impressive 18 metres by 9.5 metres and it is one of the largest in Europe. There is a lot more than just 400 species of fish to see as there are simulated hurricanes and South Sea storms to experience

The aquarium is open every day for all of July and August from 10am to 10pm. The rest of the year the opening times are Sunday to Thursday 10am to 7pm and Friday and Saturday 10am to 8pm. Expect to pay €15,50 for adults, children's tickets vary between €7.50 and €12.50 but there are various ticket combinations available.

Karting & Bowling

The 40 lane bowling alley is great fun and for small children there are 6 specially designed lanes. There is also a soft play area, a billiards room and an indoor karting track with a bar and snack bar for recharging your batteries. The opening hours are from noon everyday until 1am Sunday to Thursday, 2am Friday and 3am Saturday. The price for the Karting is €15 and the bowling varies between €4 and €7.

Ice Skating

There is plenty of room to skate and not just on flat ice while the DJ plays the top sounds to keep things moving. The ice rink is unusual as it has a special area with a slope as well as a tunnel to skate through lit with multi-coloured bulbs.

In school holidays the ice rink is open every night and some mornings. The rest of the year it is closed Tuesday mornings but open morning and afternoon and then three nights a week. The ice rink does close for a lunch break. Skate hire is around €3 and the admission price is €5 for adults and €4 for under 16's.

Odysseum Activities

If all the above isn't enough there is a climbing wall to test stamina and strength and a mini-park for young children. For a special meal out take the children to the Pirates Paradise, a themed restaurant or listen to some live music at the Irish pub most nights. There are 16 restaurants to choose from so there is bound to be something to suit everyone.

Fabre Museum

39 Boulevard Bonne Nouvelle
Montpellier
Tel: +33 4671 48300
www.museefabre.montpellier-agglo.com/

In 1802 a donation to the city of 30 paintings became the basis of a small museum in the town housed in a hotel. Several years later in 1825 François-Xavier Fabre generously added a large amount of his works to the collection and the Hôtel Massillian was duly refurbished and was renamed as the Fabre Museum.

Other artists soon followed Fabre's example and by 1877 nearly one thousand items had been donated by Alfred Bruvas, Jules Canonge and Jules Bonnet-Mel from their own private collections.

From 2003 to 2007 the museum had a 21st century makeover costing 61.2 million and is now classified by the French Ministry of Culture as a Museum of France. The museum building is just a short stroll along a tree-lined avenue from the Place de la Comédie and Gare St. Roch and is easy to find.

The museum is open every day except Mondays from 10am to 6pm. Ticket prices vary widely for everyone, depending on residency, age and whether it is a guided tour or not. All the prices are on the website.

Montpellier Zoo

50 Avenue Agropolis,
Montpellier
Tel: +33 4996 14550
www. zoo.montpellier.fr/

Montpellier zoo is to the north of the city and there is a really varied selection of animals. There are zebras, giraffes, rhinos plus a mixture of South American birds and African mammals. The zoo makes for a great day out as the admission is free unless you want to visit the Amazonian greenhouse. The greenhouse is fascinating and the seven climatic zones are home to more than 500 animals including tarantulas, piranhas and snakes. To make them feel at home there is an artificial rainstorm created every two hours.

The park itself is beautiful even if you don't visit the greenhouse with plenty of walks and a 20 hectare nature reserve. Access by car and public transport easy but it is quite a long walk from the nearest tram line stop at St. Eloi but there is a connecting bus to the zoo

An adult ticket is €6.50 and children pay €3. The zoo is open from 9.30am until 6.30pm from 1st April until 30th September. The rest of the year the zoo opens at 10am and closes an hour or so earlier. All the hours are on the zoo website.

Château Flaugergues

1744 Avenue Albert Einstein
Montpellier,
Tel: +33 4995 26637
www.flaugergues.com

There are many follies in the Languedoc-Roussillon area and the Château de Flaugergues near Montpellier is just one of them. The wealthy merchants and aristocrats who built the castles were servants to the French king and they filled their beautiful homes with priceless furniture and tapestries.

Etienne de Flaugergues bought his land in 1696 and starting building but it took him 45 years to complete the château. In 1811 the estate was purchased by the Boussairolles family and it was this family that designed the gardens and orangery. The gardens cover nearly four hectares and are immaculate with neatly clipped box hedges, a vineyard and some very English- style flower gardens.

There is an on-site restaurant serving excellent cuisine in beautiful surroundings. The Folia restaurant is open from 12 noon until 2.30pm. Local produce is used and the menu is planned according to the season.

An accompanied visit of the château and gardens cost €9.50 for adults and €7 for children and concessions. There are different visits with different prices available for just the gardens only, and/or the wine cellars and a wine and cheese tasting session. Château Flaugergues gardens are open all year round, apart from Sundays and bank holidays from 9.30am to 12.30pm and 14.30 to 7pm.

In June, July and September the gardens open on Sunday and bank holidays but only in the afternoon. The interior of the château is open in June, July and September from 2.30pm to 7pm but not on Mondays. The rest of the year is by appointment only, except for on Sundays.

Royal Square of Peyrou

Montpellier
Tel: +33 4676 06060

The wide tree-lined promenade of the Royal Square of Peyrou is a favourite place for the locals to stroll and enjoy the air. The statue of Louis XIV on horseback is a focal point along with the Arch de Triomphe and the Château d'Eau. Under the 18th century aqueduct on a Saturday there is a second-hand book market and organic food stalls. The belvedere was completed in 1774 to celebrate the accession of Louis XVI to the throne and offers a panoramic view of the city.

The square is very pretty when the sun goes down and the city lights are sparkling. In the months of June and July the opening hours are 7am to midnight. The rest of the year the park opens at 7am but closes at 9.30pm, and slightly earlier in November, December and January at 8pm. Admission is free.

St. Peter's Cathedral

6 Rue l'Abbé Marcel Montels
Montpellier
Tel: +33 4676 60412
www.catholique-montpellier.cef.fr/

Montpellier Cathedral is the seat of the archbishops of Montpellier as well as being a national monument of France. The cathedral started life as a humble church attached to the Saint Benoît monastery founded in 1364. The church was elevated to cathedral status in 1536 due to the see of Maquelonne being transferred to Montpellier on the orders of King François I.

The approach to the front of the cathedral is striking. The front of the 14th century building has two rocket-shaped pillars each measuring 4.55 metres in diameter. These pillars support an impressive arched canopy of stone which leads into the cathedral.

The war between the Catholics and Protestants in the 16th century meant the cathedral suffered severe damage but it was rebuilt again the following century. The interior reveals a magnificent organ case and a stunning vaulted nave. In the right-hand transept the 17th century altarpiece is a delight for the eyes and well worth a visit.

One of the well-known Protestant painters of the 17th century was Sébastien Bourdon who was born in Montpellier. He spent much of his life in Paris but from 1657 to 1658 he returned to Montpellier to paint The Fall of Simon the Magician. The painting was hung over the main altar in the cathedral and is still there today.

The cathedral is open Monday to Saturday 9am to 7pm and Sunday 9am to 1pm, Admission is free.

Château de La Mosson

Route De Lodève
Montpellier
Tel: +33 4676 06060

Joesph Bonnier was a rich banker in Montpellier and to display his wealth he purchased the Mosson estate in 1710 and work on the château started in 1723. The building was completed by 1729 and the Mosson family lived in the sumptuous château with its lavishly decorated gardens for many years. The Bonnier wealth didn't last and the family went bankrupt leaving the château to be used as factories and workshops for silks, soaps and dyes.

The city of Montpellier acquired the estate in 1982 and for many years has been trying to restore the building and gardens to their former glory. The 15 hectare park of the estate is well worth exploring along with the remains of the building itself as there is a lot of history in the area. The gardens are a public park now with free admission. The only reminder now of Bonnier's folly is the Baroque fountain and some of the statues.

Museum of Anatomy & the Faculty of Medicine

3 Rue Delmas
Montpellier
Tel: +33 4670 24769

A visit to Montpellier would not be complete without taking time to see the amazing, and sometimes gruesome, collections in the Museum of Anatomy. It is the largest anatomy museum in France and the exhibits rival the similar museum La Specola in Florence.

Montpellier has a long history associated with medicine and along with Strasbourg and Paris was one of the first cities in 1340 authorised to dissect corpses. By 1795 the new School of Medicine had opened in the city and in 1798 it was decided that to pass their exams all the doctors had to present an anatomical work. This rule remained in force until 1940. Meanwhile a very large collection of pieces were building up in the dean's office and in 1851 a new building was built to display this impressive collection.

Visitors today with nerves of steel and a strong stomach can go into the 15 metre high and 60 metre long gallery to see the rotten and diseased organs along with mummies and sections of the brain. Formalin has long been the preservative of choice for specimens in years gone by and there are plenty to see here. Deformed foetuses float eerily round in their glass wombs while skulls grin down at their audience while seeing nothing from sightless eye sockets.

Despite the marvels of modern technology that can take photographs and scans of inside the human body there is still a certain educational value in seeing the actual parts.

There are nearly 6,000 items in the collection and a two hour tour is organised by the Montpellier Tourist Office in Place de la Comédie to see this exceptional site of medical history. All the information is on the tourist office website; www.ot-montpellier.fr/en/

Montpellier Historical Centre

Between the Place de la Comédie and the Peyrou Arch are the old quarters of Montpellier. Due to its original shape the Place de la Comédie is known to the locals as l'OEuf (the Egg) and the ovoid shape comes from being built on the ramparts that surrounded the ancient city. The pedestrianised square with its central statue of the Three Graces is one of the largest city squares in Europe.

The narrow, winding streets of the city centre hide many little shops, cafés and restaurants and you can enjoy the simple pleasure of walking and listening to birdsong rather than the hum of traffic. There are numerous places to get a cup of decent French coffee accompanied by a delicious pastry of two, or maybe a glass of wine and some snails or frogs legs.

Many of the buildings in the city centre date back to medieval times but some were improved between the 16th and 18th centuries. Take time and admire the architecture of the beautiful private homes, some of the façades are remarkable and wrought iron gates lead through to hidden courtyards and staircases.

Henri Prades Museum

390, route de Pérols
34970 Lattes
Montpellier
Tel: +33 4679 97720
www.museearcheo.montpellier-agglo.com/

It was only by luck that the ancient city of Lattara was found after a field was deep-ploughed in 1963. Henri Prades along with the Painlevé Archaeological Group (GAP) decided that the site showed great promise for studying Gallic civilization as it moved forward into the Roman Era.

This ancient port was active for over 800 years and many populations used Lattara as the cultural and economic centre of the western Mediterranean. Celtic populations as well as Etruscans, Romans, Greeks and Iberians all passed through as they traded their goods with other cultures.

On the edge of the site in the old Saint-Sauveur farmhouse there is more than just a museum; there is an archaeological centre, research laboratories, a library and the excavation headquarters. The museum holds the fascination collections from the archaeological digs that have taken place over the years.

To visit the museum is free on the first Sunday of every month, on other days the admission fee is €2,50. The opening hours are Monday, Wednesday, Thursday, Friday from 10am to 12 noon and 1.30pm to 5.30pm.Saturday and Sunday 2pm to 6pm. Closed on Tuesday.

Antigone District

The Antigone District lies to the east of the historical centre of Montpellier and the 36 hectare site was developed in the late 1970's to expand the city out towards the River Lez. The project became the subject of much public interest worldwide and was one of the biggest developments in France ever to be completed.

The Catalan architect Ricardo Bofill was the man given the mammoth task of designing the development. He had to include everything a new city would need from local shops and public facilities to government buildings and offices. Much of the housing is low cost and is situated in a network of plazas and tree-lined boulevards. The Esplanade de l'Europe is a very impressive curved apartment building facing the open space of the Plaza de Thessalie.

The Antigone District is worth a visit just to admire the neo-classical architecture. There are many columns, pilasters, pediments and entablatures on a gigantic scale which gives the whole area a monumental aspect.

Botanical Gardens

Boulevard Henri IV
Montpellier
Tel: +33 4676 34322
www.univ-montp1.fr

The Botanical Gardens in Montpellier were established in 1593 and are France's oldest botanical gardens. When a similar garden was created in Paris in 1626 it was modelled on the Montpellier garden.

The 4.5 hectare garden contains 500 native Mediterranean plants and about 2,100 non-native. Roughly two thirds of the plants are grown outside and the rest under glass. The garden is divided into sections making it easier to browse through your favourite plant and in the systematic garden the plants are classified by the Bentham and Hooker system.

Other sections include medical plants, palm trees, arboretum, succulents, the cold greenhouse and orangery and finally a warm greenhouse with tropical and aquatic plants.

The Botanical Gardens are looked after by the Montpellier University and open every afternoon except Monday. The garden is classified as a Historical Monument and Protected Site and admission is free.

Château de la Mogère

2235 Route de Vauguiéres
Montpellier
Tel: +33 4676 57201
www.lamogere.fr/

The Renaissance style Château de la Mogére was designed by architect Jean Giral for a Secretary of State called Fulcran Limouzin. Giral's original design is still closely adhered to and the appearance of the château has hardly changed over the centuries. Viewed from the far end of the garden the symmetry of the château is apparent against the green of the pine forest. The wide sweeping steps lead up to the house with 18 pairs of matching white shutters keeping the French sunshine out.

The château and the gardens are open to the public and there are plenty of antique paintings and family portraits to see. Jacques-Louis David, Jean Jouvenet and Hyacinthe Rigaud are just three of the artists that have contributed their work to this wonderful collection. There are many fine examples of Louis XIV and XV in the château all beautifully preserved. The gardens are very pretty especially the fountain. A number of cherubs decorate the water feature which is made out of thousands of seashells.

Access is easy to Château La Mogére as it is right next to the auto route A9 and is opposite the Odysseum. The Montpellier tramway line stops at the Oysseum which is a ten minute walk to the château.

Admission prices for the gardens and château are €6 for adults and €3 for children. For access to the gardens only it is €3 each. The opening hours are 1st June to 30th September from 2.30pm to 6.30pm every day. From 1st January to 31st May and 1st October to 31st December Château La Mogére is open Saturdays, Sundays and national holidays. Other days can be arranged by appointment.

Esplanade Charles de Gaulle

Part of any holiday in this well-known wine growing region should include some tastings. From July through to September there is a wine festival every Friday evening from 6.30pm to 11.30pm in the Esplanade de Charles de Gaulle. For €5 you get a wine glass to keep and three tasting tickets. Wander round the 35 stalls and soak up the ambience while deciding which wine to sample. There are food stalls as well and many people buy a few snacks then sit and relax on the grass listening to the live band.

Recommendations for the Budget Traveller

Places to Stay

Montpellier Hostel

Rue des Ecoles Laiques
Impasse Petite Corraterie
Montpellier
Tel: +33 4676 03222

The Montpellier is a 94 bed hostel right in the heart of the city, close to all the shops, bars and major attractions. The room price includes breakfast and the hostel offers free Wifi, pool table, football table and has its own bar. There is a storage room at the hostel for luggage and cycle hire is available close by.

Different size dorms are available, both single sex and mixed. Prices are from around €20 per person per night.

Les Arbousiers

1022 Rue de Las Sorbes
Montpellier
Tel: +33 6151 06739
www.dauzac.org/

Les Arbousiers is a family run guest house that is close to all the attractions that Montpellier has to offer. There are five bedrooms, some with access to the large balcony. There are no ensuite rooms but ample bathrooms and showers for sharing.

The house is set in a pleasant garden full of flowers and trees and is ideal for a peaceful stay but still handy for the centre. There is free car parking outside on the street and the tram stop is close by for a quick trip into the city centre.

Expect to pay from €30 per person per night which includes breakfast with the family. Dinner with the family can be booked in advance and it is a good way to practice your French. Don't worry if you are not fluent as the father speaks very good English.

La Farigoule

13 av du General Grollier
Pignan
Montpellier
Tel: +33 4672 70894
www.lafarigoule34.com/

A few kilometres away from Montpellier is the La Farigoule guest house. The house is in the typical Languedoc style and was originally a wine-growers house. There are only three rooms, all with one double bed and one single bed. The rooms have en-suite facilities and are all beautifully decorated.

Prices per night for three people sharing a room are €80 per room, two sharing €62 per room and for one person €52 per room. A light continental breakfast is included. There is a very pretty terrace with honey coloured stone walls and tumbling flowers where breakfast is served when the weather permits. In the colder months there is a pleasant dining room with a large fireplace.

La Vagance

155 rue des Escarceliers
Montpellier
Tel: +33 4674 02935
www.lavagance.fr/

La Vagance is set in a tranquil suburb of Montpellier in lush gardens with lots of palm trees framing the south facing breakfast terrace. There are two rooms, the Iris Room with a double bed and the Grand Cèdre with twin beds. Both rooms are spacious with comfortable beds and en-suite showers. Breakfast is included and rates are from €37.50 per person per night for two people sharing. There are special rates for three-night breaks and longer stays.

Sweet Home 34

15 rue Claude Chappe
Montpellier
Tél : +33 4995 19932
www.sweet-home34.fr/

Sweet Home 34 guest house is only a short distance from the historic centre of Montpellier and all the beautiful architecture that the city offers. Closer to this relaxing guest house are the clean and modern lines of the Antigone District with its shops, bars and restaurants to enjoy.

There are five rooms in Sweet Home 34 to choose from, some with king size beds, some with doubles. Some of the rooms have private facilities but not all of them. All the rooms have air conditioning and Wifi. The prices are from €55 per person per night for two people sharing a room and this includes breakfast.

Places to Eat & Drink

Playfood

16, Boulevard Louis Blanc
Montpellier
Tel: +33 4342 26152
www.playfood.fr

For a different dining experience find Playfood on the gentle curving Boulevard Louis Blanc, it isn't hard to find as one of the tram lines runs right down the centre of the street. The restaurant inside has a modern feel and there are wooden chairs and tables outside for dining al fresco.

Playfood serves food in verrines. Verrines are small thick glasses that contain food rather than liquids. There is a wide variety of hot or cold, sweet or savoury treats to choose from including a good vegetarian selection. All the verrines are sold individually and cost around €2-€2.50 each. Playfood is open from Tuesday to Saturday from 7.30pm to midnight.

Le P'tit Mas

30, avenue Pierre d'Adhemar
Montpellier
Tel: +33 4675 72581

The snack bar and café is popular with locals for its cosy and friendly atmosphere and good food. Some of the house specialties are grilled prawns and cuttlefish, oysters and a selection of delicious sounding salads. Le P'tit Mas is open from 8am to 10.30pm all week except for Saturday evenings.

The café is family friendly and groups are welcome. A decent meal and drinks is around €15 while the menu of the day is €11. There is a large terrace outside with a nice view where you can sit and watch the word pass by.

Le Pescator

23 pl. du Nombre d'Or
Montpellier
Tel: +33 4671 32916
www.restaurant-lepescator-montpellier.fr

The brightly coloured bar complete with portholes when you enter Le Pescator sets the nautical theme for your meal of freshly caught fish and shellfish. With jazz music playing gently in the background you can ponder over the á la carte or daily menus.

The three course menu costs €30 and has enticing dishes like Monkfish Provençal, Smoked Red Scottish Salmon and Bream or for non-fish eaters there is a Fillet of Beef. If you are in hurry just have a quick meal of Mussels and Chips for €14.

Le Pescator is open every day for lunch and dinner, the restaurant has air-conditioning and there is a shady terrace for eating out on summer days.

Pain et Cie

4 Place Jean Jaurès
Montpellier
Tel: +33 4676 02435
www.painetcompagnie.fr/

Pain et Cie is a great place to eat right in the heart of the city and to meet people. In the centre of the restaurant is a large communal table where you can join in and get to know locals and visitors alike. There are three smaller rooms with seating for a more intimate experience as well as a large shaded terrace. The restaurant serves good home cooked food in huge portions all with a regional flavour. Try the breaded and fried cheese wheel as a starter and you might not want a main course.

The waitresses are fast and efficient and do speak a little English. Pain et Cie is open all day seven days a week for breakfast, lunch and dinner. They also sell a range of breads, jams and spices to takeaway.

Times Café

7-9 Rue des Teissiers
Montpellier
Tel: +33 4675 49842

The Times Café celebrated its tenth anniversary in 2011 and is considered to be one of the best wine bars in the city. It is a super place to meet friends and enjoy a selection of French wines accompanied by a selection of bite-sized snacks.

Tasty French bread with olives, sun-dried tomatoes plus foie gras and fig jam are just some of the items on the menu. There is a wide selection of platters to sample with fish, meat and vegetarian options. Opening hours are Monday to Saturday from 6.30pm to 1am.

Places to Shop

Les Halles Castellane

Place Castellane
Montpellier

To get a feel for how the French do their shopping have a wander round Les Halles Castellane. Lose yourself in the hustle and bustle of the daily market and enjoy all the tempting aromas of fresh bread mingling with espresso coffee as well as the butchers, fishmongers and fruit and vegetable stalls.

Stock up on some cold meats and cheese, pop in a bottle of wine and some crusty bread and go for a picnic. Montpellier has some beautiful open spaces to lunch in the fresh air. For an alternative there are pizza stalls and octopus pies from the little city of Sète close by. The market is open Monday to Saturday from 7.30am to 7.30pm, Sundays and bank holidays from 7.30am to 3pm.

Peyrou Plaza

Jardins du Peyrou
Montpellier
Tel: +33 6227 70721

This is a great place for bargain hunters and the perfect place to spend a Sunday morning. The antique dealers and secondhand stalls can hide all sorts of undiscovered treasures. There are decorative items for the home, used and old books plus fancy and unusual goods are all there waiting to be found.

There is usually live music playing and there are places to eat, drink and soak up the atmosphere. Be there early to get the best bargains, the market opens at 7.30am to 2pm and there is free car parking in the Arceaux nearby.

Images du Demain

10, rue de la Vieille
Montpellier
Tel: +33 4676 62345
www.carterie-encadrement-montpellier.com/

Many visitors like to take a painting or print home as a reminder of their holiday. This is the shop to find just that souvenir and the choice is vast. Be prepared to spend a while searching the walls of the alley outside the shop for the right picture.

There are maps, prints, postcards, drawings and posters in all sizes and with prices to suit all budgets. The friendly and helpful staff will do their best to find the best picture to suit your taste. Images du Demain is open Monday to Saturday from 9.30am to 7.30pm.

Le Boutik'R

41 Boulevard Bonne Nouvelle
Montpellier
Tel: +33 4676 63593
www.leboutikr.fr/

A visit to Le Boutik'R must be part of any holiday in Montpellier. The city as well as the Languedoc Roussillon region has many talented arts and crafts workers and examples of their work can be found here.

The shop opened in 2008 in a beautiful old mansion with high, vaulted ceilings and offers a range of home ware and linen as well as a variety of home produced food and wine.

The owners are passionate about quality and authenticity and the shop has the Quality Hérault label as many of the items stocked are local to the area. Le Boutik'R is open 10am to 7pm Tuesday to Saturday and 1pm to 6pm on Sunday. The shop is very close to the Fabré Museum and Place du Comédie.

Etat d'Ame

12 Rue en Gondeau
Montpellier
Tel: +33 4676 07920

An explosion of colour awaits you as soon as you enter Etat d'Ame. The shop sells china, brightly coloured linens, and novelty items like flattened bottle-tops made into chandeliers. The long table that greets you is full of Polish handmade cups, bowls and plates; none of which match but that is part of the charm.

To add to this rainbow tea party there are vintage toys and old cinema chairs imported from India. To browse among these items Etat d'Ame is open Monday to Saturday 9am to 6pm.